Fo

Poems On Belonging, Healing and Overcoming Trauma.

Eli Ash

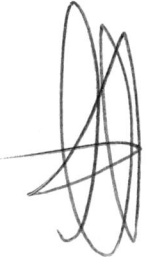

Copyright

© Eli Ash, 2025
All rights reserved.

No part of this publication may be reproduced, stored in a retrieval system, or transmitted in any form or by any means, electronic, mechanical, photocopying, recording, or otherwise, without the prior written permission of the author, except for brief quotations used in reviews or critical articles.

This is a work of creative nonfiction. The poems, quotes, and reflections are based on personal experiences and emotions. Some names and identifying details may have been changed to protect the privacy of individuals.

First Edition
Cover design by Eli Ash
Printed in the United Kingdom
Published by Amazon

'Illegitimi non carborundum'
I didn't let you grind me down

A collection of poems, quotes, and reflections,

offering a voice to the lived experience of foster care.

Section One: During

Part One: The Weight of Small Thing

LAC (Looked After Child)	1
Goodbye	5
Small thing	9

Part Two: Rebellion & Resistance

Purple (A Teenage Hair Dye Story)	12
I hate Math's	14
Think you know me	16

Part Three: Love and Connection

Hers and His	20
My beautiful	21

Part Four: Anguish and Silence

No man	23
SS	25
Faith	26
Turn back time	27

Section Two: After

Part One: Scars & Shadows

Before and After	30
Younger Self	32
Milestones	34

What You Did to Me	35
Feel	36
This Side of My Skin	37
Eggshells and Hauntings	38
Foster Parent	39
For Me	40
Demons Blooming	42
Hold The Quiet	45
Part Two: Family's Tangled Web	
Mother	47
Terms and Conditions	48
Liar	49
People	50
Respect	51
Three Sisters	52
Fact	54
Pride and Disappointment	55
Why?	56
Trauma Cycle	58
Trying to Fix You	60
Sisters	61
I Threw My Toys Out The Pram	62
Part Three: Echoes Of Loss	
Outlive Me	64

Graveyard	65
World	66
Anxiety	67
Daydreaming	70
Cheeto	71

Part Four: Flickers Within

Booklover	73
Dreams	74
Love	75
Souls Mirror	76
M	77
In Poetry	79
Silence Between The Heartbeats	80
ILY	81
Saint	83
Charm	84
Dreamers	85
Tea	86

Part Five: Masks And Mirrors

Shapeshifter	88
Social Media	90
Burden	92
Feel Like a Child	93

Part Six: Heathens and Gods

Morrigan	95
Death	96
GOD	98
Luna	100
Night	101

Part Seven: Trials of Motherhood

To Have You	103
Postpartum Depression	106
Summer Holidays	110

Section One: During

Trigger warnings:

Violence, physical abuse, child neglect, death, grief, rage, blasphemy, emotional distress, mental health issues (including depression, anxiety, dyscalculia), addiction, alcohol misuse, self-harm, suicide, abandonment, family breakdown, social services involvement, loss, bullying, and identity struggle.

Part One: The Weight of Small Things

LAC (Looked After Child)

Move on and move in.

Cried out, Cried loud.

Different people.

Different houses.

Different plans.

Same life.

Same past.

Same turnout.

She's just a LAC girl.

That's her,

That's them, the Looked After Child.

Isolated, alone. Labelled.

That's her

the alcoholic, the mother.

They whisper,

"The poor girls...

What a life."

Poor mum.

"Hi, hello, how are you?"

"Welcome to our home."

A few weeks pass.

"You're going back home."

Bye.

See you later.

Goodbye.

New home.

New people.

New area.

Same life.

Same pain.

Same cycle.

Forever home,

Forever people.

Taken away.

Ripped away.

Forced away.

Phone calls

Photos gone.

Contact centres.

Belongings stuffed

in black bags.

Tick.

Tick.

Box ticked.

Same life.

Same past.

Same turnout.

Goodbye

One slurred line.

One safe hug.

Five bottles down,

then one empty shrug.

Three hospital trips.

One brand-new dress.

One tidy room

To hide the mess.

One cinema trip.

One pair of shoes.

One visit to the seaside,

to avoid the blues.

One hit.

One slap.

One bruise she hides.

Nine more bottles

then the sister guides.

One hospital trip.

Three broken, confused girls.

One visiting hour

in a world that swirls.

One ready meal.

Three quiet smiles.

One mended heart,

For a little while.

Nine bottles more.

One house on fire.

One more trip,

then a family for hire.

Soon

Nine bottles.

One slurred line.

One broken family.

One visiting hour.

One last breath,

And a wilted flower.

One funeral.

One hundred cries.

Three girls,

three lives,

one word:

Goodbye.

Small Thing

Just a small thing, it stands

Chubby legs, fingers, hands.

A bruise, a black eye,

A thump that lands.

The shadow black,

An empty rose.

One investigation.

One visit home.

One happy smile.

One broken soul.

Tears fall.

Crying.

Bang goes the poll.

Silence

Not a stir in sight.

Just a small thing, it lays—

cold chubby legs, fingers, hands.

A bruise.

A broken back.

A thump that lands.

The shadow black,

An empty rose.

Part Two: Rebellion & Resistance

Trigger warnings: Violence, emotional and verbal abuse, trauma, neglect, mental health struggles (including depression, anxiety, post-natal depression), rage, grief, death and loss, suicide and suicidal thoughts, abandonment, family breakdown, addiction and alcohol misuse, self-harm, feelings of isolation, and emotional distress.

Purple (A Teenage Hair Dye Story)

Violet here.

Purple there.

Hair dye

Everywhere.

A streaked ear,

A-stained floor.

"Don't you dare!"

I did it.

(It's my hair.)

They roll their eyes,

I own the glare

I like my

Creative flair.

Now I'm grounded.

I feel kind of bad.

But deep inside?

I'm still a little glad.

I hated to burst their bubble,

but I think I look cool

they say it's a phase.

I say it's a rule.

I'm not in trouble

I'm just being me.

Using my body

as a sketchpad,

wild and free.

I Hate Math's

Numbers, letters, and tired old rhymes

Ugly words in perfect lines.

For an English dictionary, I pine.

So fuck off with your "corresponding line."

Oh, how I hate education:

Droning teachers, endless tasks.

Teens in quiet resignation

We hide behind our painted masks.

Numbers and letters just don't mix!

Right angles? Circles? What cruel tricks.

My maths brain's broken please, just nix it.

I'd rather drown in shades of lipstick.

I hate maths.

I can't add. I can't tell the time.

So leave me here,

In English rhyme.

Dyscalculia.

Think You Know Me

They think they know me

Just what you want

A story, a label,

A box to tick.

But they don't have a clue.

So shut your mouth!

Don't say a word!

You don't know me

You never will.

So shut your mouth!

Don't say a word!

They say what I want to hear.

Pretend to care.

Act like they see me.

They've heard *about* me.

But not one of them

Knows who I am.

I'm not a file.

I'm not a case.

I'm not a page in your clipboard maze.

So shut your mouth.

Don't say a word.

You don't know me

you never will.

Don't.

Say.

A word.

Part Three: Love and Connection

Hers and His

Midnight conversations,

Wrapped in your hold.

Changed by the good girl,

saved by the bad boy.

The boy.

The girl.

Mine.

Yours.

Hers.

His.

My Beautiful

Absent-minded rubbing

My beautiful bump.

Little hands and tiny toes,

Sealed shut eyelids

It takes away my woes.

Nervous, excited,

My feelings grow.

Two beats in one body—

You are my enlightenment.

I love you

Like clouds in the sky,

Like birds in the trees.

And I can feel

you love me too.

Part Four: Anguish and Silence

No Man

I'm just a no man.

A lonely no man.

Can't you see

I'm nobody?

But they want to see you.

Take you places

You've never been.

They say they care.

They said:

Don't be lonely.

We'll hold your hand.

Make you feel special.

We're going nowhere.

But then

They let go.

Just like the rest do.

I'm just a no man.

A lonely no man.

Can't you see

I'm nobody.

SS

I'm a person.

I'm human.

You're just a monster.

You ruined me

But I'm still here.

You bite.

You take.

But not this time.

You get nothing.

Faith

Put your faith in me.

Put your faith in me.

I'll flood your homes,

kill your children.

Still, you pray.

Put your faith in me.

Oh, you poor, poor soul

Darkening, blackening.

So, pray.

Put your faith in me.

Turn back time

Can I turn back time and make everything alright?

Can I say I'm sorry and take away your pain?

So, I can be your sun, let me be your light.

I'm so sorry I played you like a game.

So, can you forgive me? Please say you forgive me.

Section Two: After

Trigger Warnings: Violence, physical abuse, child neglect, death, grief, rage, blasphemy, emotional distress, mental health issues (including depression, anxiety, dyscalculia), addiction, alcohol misuse, self-harm, suicide, abandonment, family breakdown, social services involvement, loss, bullying, and identity struggle.

Part One: Scars & Shadows

Before and After

There's only before and after,

Every day,

My life revolves around those moments.

I can't recall what I had for dinner,

But I can walk you step by step through those events.

My life doesn't move forward,

Not in a line,

Not even in waves.

It orbits in circles

Around the before,

My existence is trapped in the after.

I don't want to be so consumed,

So self-centred on my memories,

But it's woven in my makeup,

Etched in my genes.

Neglect hardened me,

Exposure made me resilient,

Verbal abuse shaped my kindness.

I don't know who I am without it

Twelve years on,

Before

And

After.

Younger Self

I saw my younger self today.

I wanted to tell them it would be okay,

But I knew they wouldn't believe me.

I saw my younger self today.

I wanted to give them a hug,

Instead, I clasped their shoulders,

Armed them with advice sharp as knives,

Gave them truths that stung like a thousand bees.

They nodded and thanked me.

They saw themselves ten years from now

Knowing they'd have to bite, crawl, and scream their

way through.

Nothing but grit and truth.

Because kids in care don't get to dream,

Shouldn't hope.

Life shows us early what reality means.

Milestones

I hold wisdom you'll never find,

You enrage and blind my mind.

You grew fine, you took your time,

While I'm stuck chasing every line.

Behind the steps I should have known,

Running late on every milestone.

What You Did to Me

The sudden drop when you miss a stair,

That raw, cold fear you're forced to bear.

The near miss of a speeding car,

The tremors shaking after too much coffee, far.

Sweat pooling deep from summer's heat,

The queasy churn just before defeat.

Cheeks burning red as you silently beg,

Legs strong enough to flee, then weak when you're safe in bed.

Feel

I feel nothing.

Until I do.

Until I feel everything.

Until I become it.

Monstrous and twisted.

With widened jaws and a slithering tongue

Consuming in hate and speaking poisons.

This Side of My Skin

I have freckles on this side of my skin,

Constellations you can trace with your finger.

I have stretch marks on this side of my skin,

Canyons and valleys, maps my children did begin.

I have swollen keloids, raised like tumours.

Of twisted, weeping flesh...

Firing wrong, thoughts tangled, nerves enmeshed.

The skin won't show the pain that stays,

The mind still lost in twisted maze.

A war beneath, no blood, no stain

Just echoes pulsing through the brain.

I wish this side of skin would show.

The scorched remains that burn below.

Eggshells And Hauntings

I know the feel of eggshells beneath my feet

A fragile path I walk, uncertain, discreet.

Haunted by you still living,

Shadows of a past unforgiving.

Foster Parent

Emotional torture

From someone meant to save us.

The skin on my hands is blistering,

Her mind is withering.

If we told them what you did,

Would that be a bad thing?

Bickering echoes in the hallway,

Pitting us against each other.

Emotional torture

From someone meant to save us.

For Me

For me

Little me sitting on the stairs,

Listening to the shouts.

For me

Younger me saying hello

All over again.

For me

Teenage me who wants to pummel and cry.

For me

Teenage me finding comfort

In disappointment.

For me

Another second chance.

For me

Desperate for your time, your love.

For me

Do not forget.

It will not change.

For me

I'm sorry.

Demons Blooming

Demons are blooming

Pounding, pacing, separating.

Demons are rooting,

But the flowers keep blooming.

Boxes, books, bags

Demons root beneath hemlocks' gloom.

Hold me tight.

Nice and warm.

I've been dug up, re-rooted

My flowers need pruning.

Why do I feel this?

Hold me tight.

Nice and warm.

Ashes in pills,

Pills and powders.

Demons rooting,

Yellow bells are blooming.

Smile and hide.

Hold me in a tight embrace.

Don't look into my eyes.

You'll see the truth in my face.

Why is it so easy

To be taken over?

Why is it so easy

To lose my mind?

Demons seep in

while laurels keep blooming.

One thing remains:

boxes, books, bags,

Furniture, folks, future.

Demons root

flowers bloom.

I need the pills to feel happy.

A tight embrace to feel safe

When I'm so down.

All of this.

Just for a house.

Hold The Quiet

I hold the quiet, clutch it tight,

Like mother mourning through the night.

Dark and anguished, shadows creep,

A silence heavy, vast, and deep.

I hold it close like lover's touch,

Soft caresses that hurt so much.

The quiet smiles, a ghostly guide,

Consumed my soul, no life inside.

Part Two: Family's Tangled Web

Mother

What is a good mother?

My model's broken, missing weeks at a time.

So, I became my own design.

I want my kids strong, but not from borrowed pain,

Resilient, but not forged in hate's flame.

Kind, but learned from love, not blame.

But how do I teach that?

When I lead like Queen Elinor,

See the world like Mother Gothel,

Cautious like Maleficent's lore.

Terms and Conditions

There's something to be said

About a man who makes you chase.

Chase their pride in you,

Their love for you,

Their hope for you.

Instead, you get

Their terms to be proud of you,

Conditions to show their love,

Small print

Of their hope for you.

Liar

Liar Liar

Hearts on fire

Your tongue is

Dirty and full of fire.

People

I don't have a favourite place,

I have favourite faces.

I don't have a house or a dome,

I have my person, my true home.

They are my safe and quiet space,

My favourite in every place.

Respect

It chipped away like paint,

Hiding cracks beneath the faint.

It settled deep inside my skin,

Refused to leave, refused to thin.

Lost with every stumble, every bottle drained,

Goodbye and hello, as my sister's skin stained.

A kernel remained from the sweet little girl,

But the woman inside hurled it to whirl.

For the daughter no longer respected the mum

A bond broken, a silence struck dumb

Three Sisters

Three sisters

One was left,

Two were taken,

A bond both torn and shaken.

Three sisters

The eldest abrasive,

The middle blunt and black,

The youngest justice, feeling every crack.

Three sisters

Victims of theft,

All left shaken,

Guarding children, their hearts unbroken.

The eldest, emotionally dismissive,

The middle splits with a fracturing crack,

The youngest steers with vision clear,

Holding life's motion on her track.

Three sisters

Forever bound,

In loss and love,

Their strength profound.

Fact

Broken children

In grown bodies

Miming their parents' lives

Pride And Disappointment

I still cower under the weight of gaining your pride

And shrivel under your disappointment.

Why?

"Why?" I would ask.

"It is what it is."

"Why?"

"Because I said so."

"Why?"

"I don't know."

"Why?"

"I couldn't stop."

"Why?"

"If I could change it, I would."

"Why?"

"It was because of my trauma."

"Why?"

"I was wrong."

"Why?"

"You didn't deserve that."

"Why?"

"I was in denial, immature, and scared."

"Wh—oh. Okay. But you were meant to take care of me. How? Why? Why? Why? Why? Why? Why? Why?"

"I know. I'm sorry."

Trauma Cycle

She didn't mean to hurt me

But she was traumatized.

And her trauma

Bled to me.

The cycle

Went round

And round.

She loved

The only way she knew

Or at least,

She tried to.

It didn't matter

If I got hurt.

I just wished

She'd say

She was sorry.

Trying To Fix You

I wish I could have cried

But my mum was always crying instead.

It was a change

Forced on a child.

It didn't make me stronger.

I used to say

I'd use my one wish

To make my mum sober.

But a child

Cannot fix

A parent's pain.

Sisters

Suffered and scraped,

Still, we grew.

I always looked up to you.

Still do,

Now at twenty-five.

You carried the load.

So we could survive.

Everyone's got their

Opinions and views

But they'd die

In our borrowed shoes.

Still going strong,

After all we've been through

I Threw My Toys Out The Pram

The text read, *"I'm sorry I threw my toys out the pram."*

But I didn't believe it, your words came like a sham.

You said you'd love to catch up

But all I saw was selfish thirst

To refill your empty cup.

You left a voice message, called me a selfish cunt

I laughed to stop the tears, hid pain behind a front.

I kept coming back, hoping you'd rearrange,

But your voice was scratching, itching, maddening, and

Strange.

Doing the same thing, expecting change, is insane.

So I walked away for good, carrying all my pain.

The text read, *"I'm sorry I threw my toys out the pram."*

I blocked it. Reported it as spam.

Part Three: Echoes Of Loss

Outlive Me

For those who outlive us

Know I tried.

Me and many others,

Drops into the ocean wide.

We slowed, we scaled,

Became loud, became wise.

Please know I tried

For my children, yours, our skies.

Reduced, reused, recovered what could be saved,

Drops in an ocean,

A needle in a haystack paved.

For those who outlive us

I promise, I tried.

Graveyard

Beneath the earth, wrapped tight in mist,

Echoes of childhood laughter twist.

A tombstone reads: *Here lie the nearly, the should-*

haves,

Lost within the swirling, sombre drifts.

Back and forth, I wander and sway,

Fraying slowly in this graveyard of yesterday.

World

The world is grey and dull,

hail a bitter bite.

Wind blows sharp

People wrapped in tarp.

The town is streaked with grey,

Crumbled concrete, slate.

Gutters gush, lights blink.

Dreary, deadly nights.

The world served cold,

Right on your plate.

Anxiety

Pounding, crushing

It's straining to get out.

Surrounding me,

Creeping throughout.

It's coming faster now,

Sharp like a knife

Splits in my chest,

Rising to life.

Whispers in my ear,

Kisses me to sleep.

Sharper now,

Rooted deep.

In my fingers,

My heart,

My brain,

My chest

Skin and bones

Whittling down,

No time to rest.

Cackling, clapping

In wicked glee.

Grappling with it,

Trying to get free.

Take deep breaths.

Trace it with your finger.

Shake yourself down.

Don't let it linger.

The thing huffs

And sits down

To wait

A monster,

Subsided

No longer

Crushed

Under the weight.

Daydreaming

Sometimes I dream of getting hurt,

Or worse—my loved ones crushed and burnt.

So I can set the world ablaze,

And own my fury, claim my rage.

If robbed or bruised, no one asks why,

But silence makes me wonder why.

Seen but unheard, I hold the blame,

For all that shattered my name.

Cheeto

Sometimes, if you're lucky, life gifts you a friend,

Mine came one day when loneliness seemed like it

Would never end.

I saw you familiar, from a universe apart,

A timeline where anxious souls find a brand-new start.

You laid on me one black whisker, soft and light,

Tiger-striped, with auburn patches like my mood, just

Right.

My friend in this life, the last, and the next to be,

My Cheeto, good boy forever loved by me.

Until we meet again.

Cheeto 2023–2025

Part Four: Flickers Within

Booklover

Books are gateways

Opening lives unmarked by my sadness,

Offering worlds free of my burdens.

Killers, princesses, fairies, monsters—

Lovers, pirates, enemies

Omens and prophecies

Victories and battles

Endings better than my own.

Read if you're lonely, sad, or need escape.

Dreams

Give me a meadow field.

Five ducks and a pond.

A whitewashed cottage with wooden beams.

Barefoot muddy summers.

Slow open fire winters.

A reading bench in a bay window.

Let me be free.

Love

When you are given love by broken people

You grow up to find it

In the cracks of broken men.

Souls Mirror

Writers love on paper

Artists bleed on canvases,

Singers wish in songs.

M

Weightless and crushed,

Faceless, no trust.

Drowning

It had to end.

No grounding,

Just play pretend

Phantom aberration, a ghost.

My light,

The one I love most.

You came,

Stitched my frayed heart,

A name you noticed

My new start.

Addicted to the taste of your skin,

Cocooned arms, safe to sleep.

Lulled, pulled

To your heartbeat

Intoxicated, hooked.

My one, my only—

The one that looked.

In Poetry

In English, we say,

"I'm here if you need me."

But in poetry, we say

Let your sorrows pour from you onto me.

My arms wrap you in safety,

Like a gentle summer's breeze.

Let me be the mountain

That holds you when you're weak.

Silence Between The Heartbeats

I live for moments, soft and sweet,

The space between your heart's quiet beat.

In that silence, I find my place,

Breathing slow in measured grace.

Four, six, eight, I count and wait,

Holding on to seconds late.

For in that pause, that gentle space,

Euphoria finds its quiet grace.

ILY

The way your eyes shine

A thousand galaxies sparkling

When you smile.

The unyielding strength of a mountain

When I crumble to dust.

The way I push,

And you pull

Two perfect magnets.

Pillow talks of future dreams,

Your hand in my hair

When you think I'm asleep.

The way you hug me from behind

While I'm cooking.

And I fall deeper still

When I see you

Teaching our sons

Something new.

Saint

There was a sister named Saint,

With a wild, unruly paint.

She'd rage so hard she'd faint

A delicate flower, she ain't.

Feel fear.

Make no complaint.

Charm

There was a sister named Charm,

Who went on retreats to stay calm.

She petted some goats on a farm

Didn't help though…

She broke a poor bloke's arm.

Dreamers

In the quiet of night, when children sleep,

I dream of fields where cows and sheep keep.

I dream of buses humming soft and slow,

Robins, woodpeckers in gentle flow.

Fresh baked bread and butcher's stall,

Homemade chutney, ripe tomatoes all.

Tea

When your day's gone all to shit,

And you're chomping at the bit,

Pause the chaos, take a seat,

Brew yourself a calming tea.

Its warmth soothes every taste,

Let your worries melt to space.

Part Five: Masks And Mirrors

Shapeshifter

For the girls who line their eyes with kohl,

Lips ruby red, strutting into a room.

For the boy who dons a suit

And an expensive watch.

For the perfect daughters

And perfect sons

You are a shapeshifter.

For the ones with too many parents,

Too many faces to fit into.

Arching, snapping into place

With gritted teeth

And hidden tears

You are a shapeshifter.

They call it a gift,

This way you bend.

A wonderful thing,

To change.

To fit their version of reality.

A special gift.

A shapeshifter.

What a terrible weight

Crushing your shoulders.

And still,

You pull them back

And saunter onward.

No one will know.

You are a shapeshifter.

Scrolling For Hope

Likes filling the love

Teens at the end of their rope

Forcing society to fit like a glove.

Abbreviations and a mini picture

Generational hieroglyphics

Mum has no clue about the holy scripture.

Emoji's and Tate's morbific.

What's the difference between poison and cure?

Frequency and dosage.

They need it to not be an unsocialized boor

Balancing the terms and conditions of the postage.

Scrolling for hope

Likes filling the love

Teens at the end of their rope

Forcing society to fit like a glove.

Burden

I don't want to bring you down

Tired enough, stressed enough, worried enough.

You don't need mine too.

So, I sit silent,

My heart inflating

Will it pop like a balloon?

I won't prove you right.

I won't smile while feeling your disdain

For my inability to cope.

I stay silent because I know

I am a burden.

Feel Like A Child

They say there are two wolves

One good, one bad.

Which one you feed

Matters.

But I think like a wolf,

Anger like a dragon,

Protect like a lion,

And feel like a child.

Part Six: Heathens and Gods

Morrigan

"Morrigan," I called to crows on wing,

"If strength is winning, why do I sting?"

Soft caws answered from trees so high,

A feather fell, brushed cheek, then I

Felt truth unravel, dark yet clear,

The strength I seek was always near.

Death

Oh, dear friend

So old and withered you are,

Low and crooked

My dear friend, Death.

Oh, dear friend

You're too early! Wait, was I in a car?

I can't look, it's too lurid.

You're not my friend, Death.

Oh, dear friend

Will they be at peace?

Look after them for me.

I will never forgive you, Death.

Oh, dear friend

Take me away, I have a necklace.

Silence my head. Let me be free.

Hello, Death.

Oh, dear friend

You're finally here, it's been so long.

They will be fine without me.

Nice to meet you, Death.

I'm here to escort you on

Take my arm, and I will walk with you.

I've always been here with you.

My name is Death.

GOD

I tried God once, I tried Him twice,

I prayed to find what paid the price.

I prayed to go back home again,

I prayed for light to ease the pain.

Him.

Her.

Them.

I prayed—again and then.

You answered once, you answered twice,

I found what's lost—but paid the price.

A child's heart can't hold the past,

So lost again, it never lasts.

I went back home, it wasn't safe,

Things got better, then erased.

You're wrong, you knew, you let it be,

No kind god sends a child free

To broken places, pain, and tears,

To live again those haunted years.

So I touched grass, I breathed the air,

Felt nature's pulse beyond despair.

Tuned in the world's true melody,

Found peace in a god that wasn't Thee.

Luna

You are the moon, my dear

Having phases doesn't make you less beautiful.

We are nature, my girl;

We sync with the moon,

Dance with the seasons,

And bloom where there is warmth.

Night

"Why are you so dark?" they ask in fear,

But they don't know how night became so dear.

I found no light in the harshness of day,

No peace in the sun's unforgiving ray.

The umbra whispered secrets deep and bright,

Revealing the stars, the soft safety of night.

"Why do you find trust so hard to give?"

Because flowers hide vipers, and ivy won't forgive.

The shadows taught me what eyes can't see,

In the full moon's glow, I found sanctuary.

Part Seven: Trials of Motherhood

To Have You

The journey to have you

Was long

And entirely new.

Three long days,

Tired and scared in so many ways.

I pushed and strained,

But you didn't come

I was utterly drained.

So they wheeled me down,

Your dad wore a frown,

And they cut me

Not in two,

But seven.

You came out crying,

Your fingers a little blue.

They handed you to Dad

He laughed,

Said you'd done a poo.

You screeched,

A sound like grinding metal.

"Good thing I'm half deaf," I joked.

Were you breathing?

They poked to be sure.

Routine, they said

But I wasn't so sure.

Now you're older

Still just as loud.

And of you,

I am immensely proud.

Postpartum Depression

The first time,

It was like drowning

Gasping for air,

Flailing,

Gulping as you choked.

I didn't know what it was,

What it was called,

That I was sick.

Three long months of hell.

It wasn't just one day.

You cried,

And I cried.

Dad was at work.

No one by my side.

I shouted

please stop.

Dreamed of running away,

Or drowning.

I wasn't happy,

Like a new mum should be.

It was absolutely gutting.

I held you

And slid down the stairs on my bum

In my head,

You'd fallen,

Your skull cracked open.

Every hour, I was woken.

In the living room,

The curtains stayed closed.

Stained pyjamas,

Nipples bleeding,

Body three times its size.

My midwife held my hand.

I shed my disguise.

"It's normal,

Especially after what happened," she said.

And two weeks later,

I was no longer

A fraying thread.

The dark fog lifted.

"Wow," I said.

Your dad looked up,

Alarmed.

"It's okay," I called.

"It's just my head."

It took a long time

Eighteen months, nearly

For the fog to lift,

For my thoughts to think clearly.

"What's wrong with me?" I cried.

"You have something called

postpartum depression,"

They said.

One in seven get it.

Summer Holidays

I dread it, the military prepping and diary liaising,

The endless cleaning, jam sandwiches glazing.

The breath-catching fear as they run wild and free,

Unaware of dangers no one else can see.

But they love it family days with aunties and friends,

The constant grazing that never quite ends.

Summer-long water fights soaking the floors,

Dripping through the house, leaving wet doors.

Running straight to the sea, building castles with Strangers,

Summer holidays. Chaos and changes.

THE END

Acknowledgements

I'd like to thank all the people in my life who have shown me love, my sisters, for listening patiently as I droned on about every writing project, my foster mum, Melanie, for always believing in me, pushing me forward, and giving me the kick I needed.

And my husband, who brings endless cups of tea and lets me use him as a sounding board for my restless thoughts.

To those who caused me trauma, hurt, and belittled me I hope these words reach you loud and clear, because I don't forgive you.

This book explores difficult and emotionally intense topics. If you or someone you know is struggling with any of the issues below such as grief, abuse, identity, mental health, or addiction please know you are not alone. Support is available. Below is a list of organizations that provide help, guidance, and a safe space for healing.

Emergency Help

If you are in immediate danger or need urgent support, please contact emergency services in your country (e.g. 911 in the US, 999 in the UK).

Mental Health & Emotional Distress

- **Mind** (UK) – www.mind.org.uk

- **National Alliance on Mental Illness (NAMI)** (US) – www.nami.org

- **Mental Health America** – www.mhanational.org

- **YoungMinds** (UK) – www.youngminds.org.uk

Grief, Loss, and Bereavement

- **Cruse Bereavement Support** (UK) – www.cruse.org.uk

- **The Dougy Center** (US) – www.dougy.org

- **GriefShare** – www.griefshare.org

Child Neglect, Abuse, and Family Breakdown

- **NSPCC (National Society for the Prevention of Cruelty to Children)** (UK) – www.nspcc.org.uk

- **ChildHelp National Child Abuse Hotline** (US) – www.childhelp.org

- **Family Lives** (UK) – www.familylives.org.uk

Violence, Physical Abuse, and Domestic Harm

- **Refuge** (UK) – www.refuge.org.uk

- **The National Domestic Violence Hotline** (US) – www.thehotline.org | Call: 1-800-799-7233

Suicide, Self-Harm, and Crisis

- **Samaritans** (UK) – www.samaritans.org | Call: 116 123

- **988 Suicide & Crisis Lifeline** (US) – 988lifeline.org | Call or Text: 988

- **Self Injury Support** (UK) – www.selfinjurysupport.org.uk

Addiction, Alcohol, and Substance Misuse

- **Alcoholics Anonymous (AA)** – www.aa.org

- **Narcotics Anonymous (NA)** – www.na.org

- **SMART Recovery** – www.smartrecovery.org

Bullying, Identity, and Struggle for Belonging

- **The Trevor Project** (US, LGBTQ+ Youth) – www.thetrevorproject.org

- **Ditch the Label** (Global) – www.ditchthelabel.org

- **It Gets Better Project** – www.itgetsbetter.org

Learning Differences (e.g. Dyscalculia)

- **British Dyslexia Association** (UK) – www.bdadyslexia.org.uk

- **Understood.org** (US) – www.understood.org

Faith, Doubt, and Blasphemy Struggles

- **Interfaith Network UK** – www.interfaith.org.uk

- **FaithTrust Institute** – www.faithtrustinstitute.org

Printed in Dunstable, United Kingdom